59 Ideas
for
Creative Foreign Language Teachers

TEACHER'S DISCOVERY

Thomas W. Alsop
Illustrations by Scott Earle

B29   ISBN# 0-7560-0020-3

Table of contents

Introduction-How to Use

Start your own grass roots creative teaching team using other foreign language teachers in the department as your team members. Decide when to meet and get going. You could even use some of these ideas for use in departmental meetings. This is a great opportunity to get energized! Even if you do not have team teaching, start your own grass roots team.

Hand out an activity sheet to each foreign language teacher who wants to be on this creativity team. Have them work in pairs, groups of three, four, or alone. Select a teacher to be captain-leader of the group. Teachers are to complete the activity page in their groups or alone. All come together as a large group to report on their dream lists and action plans. This discussion group should continue elaborating on the positive ideas and finalize action plans explored on the activity sheets. Be sure and emphasize that teachers are to go forward and complete their action plans. This work should be totally positive. The meeting should not turn in to a gripe session but rather an enriching, teacher centered learning activity that produces positive action plans and an improvement in teaching. CHANGE and PROGRESS are good for all of us!!!

Follow up the progress of the teaching team by observing one another in class. Comment on how the team's goals are being met.

Do as many of the 59 ideas as you can throughout the year. Keep changing!

Helpful Hints

This section provides a dream list for each creative idea. While doing each idea, you may wish to refer back to the dream lists.

Helpful Hints

Creative Idea	Dream Lists
1	puzzles, tongue twisters, verb tenses, poems, numbers, see SNAPPY SPANISH AND FRENCH STARTERS in the Teacher's Discovery catalogue
2	matching, grammar in context, situational grammar, closure
3	as songs, as poems, creative memorization, as stories, as poems, see VERBOLANDIA in Teacher's Discovery catalogue.
4	student team teaching, charades, student as teacher, in context, see GRAMMAR EXERCISES, READY TO USE SPANISH GRAMMAR, and MI LIBRO DE GRAMATICA ESPANOLA in the Teacher's Discovery catalogue
5	songs, poems, in context, games, situations see BINGO games in Teacher's Discovery catalogue
6	culture islands, realia, grammar/realia, community activities visit the FL TEACH website for methods-standard info on list serve-**http://www.cortland.edu/www/flteach/**
7	realia, picture culture, newspapers, magazines, student presentations, see FOTOCULTURA ESPAÑOLA, FAMOUS PEOPLE OF SPAIN, ROAD TRIPS THOUGH SPAIN, GESTOS EN VIVO, UNA BODA ESPAÑOLA EN EL ESCORIAL, MURAL MUSEUM, PROFESIONES DE MEXICO, AND GLOBAL SHOPPING in Teacher's Discovery catalogue.
8	situational dialogues, speeches, skits, meaningful question/answers, see SOAP OPERA STARTERS in Teacher's Discovery catalogue.
9	team meetings-lesson planning, team goals, team-5 C's as goals, teacher/administrative team sharing
10	poetry, music, dance, food, technology, student videos, learning centers
11	reading, writing, poetry, music, skits, technology, song, dance
12	students sing in groups, in pairs, songs on CD-script on OH, singing contest, game format
13	skits, readings-short stories, student presentations, letter writing, grammar points, student sharing presentations
14	charades, win-lose-draw, who am I, guess the vocabulary word, guess the verb tense
15	Teacher's Discovery catalogue, videos, posters
16	guess the verb tense, who, what, when, where, why
17	question answer sessions, comical skits, nonstop conversations using conversation cards, overhead projector-pictures

18	magazine articles/ads, newspaper articles/ads, realia, TV guide in Spanish
19	describe the situation, buy/sell something, describe person, place, thing, typical day, student diaries See MI DIARIO ESPAÑOL 1, 2, 3 and the French diary in Teacher's Discovery catalogue
20	power point presentations on culture/grammar, Internet activities, student made websites
21	Internet activities on culture, grammar on the Internet, Spanish music on the Internet, Geography on the Internet, see 44 INTERNET ACTIVITIES FOR SPANISH, FRENCH, GERMAN, INTERNET HOLIDAYS-SPANISH, MY INTERNET BOOK FOR SPANISH CLASS-Teacher's Discovery catalogue
22	teach commands in context, sing and act, dance, aerobics, read and act out stories, act out grammar-verb presentations, see Blaine Ray's books in Teacher's Discovery catalogue
23	6-7 activities per class, activities that teach 5 C's, multiple intelligences-individual differences, student centered activities, students speak Spanish the entire class in planned activities See ALSOP'S LESSON IDEA GUIDE in the Teacher's Discovery catalogue
24	grammar review each day for five minutes addressing items on the test, listening practice for five minutes using old tapes, put items of grammar on power point-student made, practice reading each day
25	AP vocabulary lists, AP grammar lists, daily practice, put on power point, put on OH, daily practice of AP listening exam tapes, AP reading practice, students make up AP notebook, Use AP Workbook
26	creative oral tests, oral tests each two weeks, reading tests, listening tests, writing tests, grammar in context
27	meet with English teachers, art teachers, social studies teachers, geography and math teachers, initiate activities, refer to EXPLORACIONES-EN CASA CON LA FAMILIA DE MONSTRUOS-Teacher's Discovery catalogue
28	oral testing, oral practice, creative skits, speeches, writing, reading, listening
29	oral testing, oral practice, creative skits, speeches, writing, reading, listening
30	paired activities, identify vocabulary, nouns, adjectives, verb tenses, main themes, dialogue from video
31	paired activities, accent improvement, pronunciation improvement, intonation practice, tongue twisters, songs, radio broadcasts-listening

32	team student teaching, student teacher centered, identify what student teacher needs and wants to do, utilize the 5 C's in teaching, create student centered classroom, culture-language, realia, community, parents, student teacher, enthusiasm journal
33	seats in pairs, seats in groups of three, groups of four, semi-circle, circle
34	list rules, apply rules, if violation enforce rules, reward good behavior, have high expectations, do not lower standards
35	greet students on entering and leaving classroom, speak in a friendly tone of voice, listen to students, talk to them about friends, TV, movies, songs, places they visit, their classes, sports, band, and music
36	talk positively, praise, do not criticize, reward students for their work, praise people, keep a praise-be positive journal
37	have advanced students teach in elementary schools, talk to school board and PTA about starting FL in elementary schools, apply for a grant to begin FL in elementary schools, talk to a university professor or the central office about getting a grant, have students do a video promoting FL study, see SNAPPY SPANISH STARTERS FOR ELEMENTARY SCHOOL in Teacher's Discovery catalogue
38	visit the middle school, talk about the FL program in your school, talk with the principal to promo FL, do a video promoting FL study
39	provide a model, real FL newspaper, divide segments for class to do, see MI PERIODICO ESPAÑOL-Teacher's Discovery catalogue.
40	let students create the FL promo brochure, work as a team, promo all foreign languages, get facts on FL study, contact ACTFL for promo ideas **www.actfl.org**
41	contact national, state and local FL organizations for ideas and dates, do a search on the Internet and get websites for organizations, do a FL talent show, celebrity week, foods
42	elect officers, plan activities in advance, plan cultural activities, games, foods, and field trips, see 101 IDEAS FOR SPANISH CLUB, Teacher's Discovery catalogue
43	contact GREAT AMERICA FUND RAISERS, do a website search for more info, contact candy companies via a websearch, sell candy, do a car wash, have a movie night in the FL, invite parents and all interested students, invite Justo Lamas to do a concert, use some of left over money for club activities, contact Justo at www.justo-lamas.net
44	create celebrity and geography bulletin boards, professions bulletin boards, mural museum, shopping, student photo bulletin boards, poetry bulletin boards, Internet bulletin boards, see Teacher's Discovery catalogue for poster sets for

SPANISH CELEBRITIES, PROFESIONES DE MEXICO, ROAD TRIPS THROUGH SPAIN, NI UN DIA SIN POESIA, INTERNET POSTERS, MURAL MUSEUM, and GLOBAL SHOPPING

45   make a list of student field trips that you wish to do, do one each semester, visit a local restaurante, go to a theater performance, a concert, try to go to activities involving your FL-culture, museums

46   contact Indiana and Wisconsin language associations to get their videos on FL promo, check ACTFL to get more info on FL video promo, check websites for AATSP to get info on Spanish promo, AATF for French, and AATG for German **www.aatsp.org www.aatg.org www.siu.edu/~aatf**

47   check with national directors of AATSP and AATF Spanish and French honor societies to start a chapter, get PTA to back this, visit AATSP and AATF websites to get info, if you have a society use students to create a promo brochure of outstanding events, members names, scholarships earned

48   invite guest speakers from your community, call the local university FL teachers and get names of guest speakers, use native speakers in the community, do song presentations, professions, language in the community, ethnic foods

49   use the National FL Standards, the 5 C's, to observe and evaluate FL teacher performance

50   talk and visit other departments, visit and observe classes in other disciplines, share ideas, have team meetings, plan interdisciplinary events

51   invite administrators to visit your FL department and classes, help teach your FL to administrators and other teacher personnel, praise administrators, thank them for their help, send them a thank you note, ask them to help with funds for special projects, ask them if grants are available, invite administrators to go as chaperones on student trips to foreign countries

52   call the parents of each of your students over the course of the school year, be patient, be honest about student's work, invite the parents to visit your class, invite the parents to help start a FL BOOSTER CLUB to raise funds for FL promo, invite parents to go as chaperones on student trips to foreign countries

53   invite business owners to speak to your FL clubs, ask local businesses to fund a FL project, invite a business to sponsor an ad in your FL newspaper, provide bilingual service to a business using your students as translators/interpreters

54   attend a FL conference in your state, regional, or national area. See ACTFL FL ANNALAS July-August edition for a list

of conferences. Also see your Teacher's Discovery catalogue for a list of conferences.

55   make a list of your most creative ideas and present one at a local, regional, or national conference, present a session on your best games, present a session on songs, learning centers, teamwork

56   contact travel companies for tour info, contact EF, NETC, BRAVO tour companies, get info from their websites, check out FL TEACH on the internet and get info from the list serve on student trips

57   work on a FL committee to improve instruction, participate in state, regional, and national leadership programs. Visit the Central States Conference website for info on the CSC leadership program-**http://centralstates.cc**

58   do an in-service on teaching communicatively, oral testing, teaching students to read, write in their FL, using cooperative learning, learning centers, technology, the INTERNET, see 44 INTERNET ACTIVITIES FOR SPANISH, FRENCH, GERMAN, INTERNET HOLIDAYS-SPANISH, MY INTERNET BOOK FOR SPANISH CLASS-Teacher's Discovery catalogue

59   pick one of your best ideas and develop it into a packet of activities, send it to Teacher's Discovery for publication consideration, do a games packet and send it to be published, do a book of your favorite activities and send it for publication consideration

Name _____

Date _____

Theme of team meeting
1 <u>Effective Warm-up Activities</u>

1. Underline how you will do your work at this meeting.
Work in pairs, work in groups of three or four, work alone

2. List below the warm-up activities you now use in class.

_____

_____

_____

3. List below your dream list of new warm-up activities that you want to use.

_____

_____

_____

_____

4. Write your action plan for including your new warm-up activities into your lesson plans. Write what, when, where, how, and why you plan to do this.

_____

_____

_____

5. Discuss with all members of the team your old and new warm-up activities. Say what your action plan is for implementing the warm-up activities into your lesson plans. Ask others for positive feedback.
<u>Instructional</u>

Team Teaching

Name _____

Date _____

Theme of team meeting
2 Writing Creative Tests

1. Underline how you will do your work at this meeting.
Work in pairs, work in groups of three or four, work alone

2. List below the creative tests that you now use in class.
_____
_____
_____

3. List below your dream list of your own teacher created tests that you want to use.
_____
_____
_____
_____
_____

4. Write your action plan for including your new creative tests into your lesson plans. Write what, when, where, how, and why you plan to do this.
_____
_____
_____
_____

5. Discuss with all members of the team your old and new teacher created tests. Say what your action plan is for implementing your own tests into your lesson plans. Ask others for positive feedback.

<u>**Instructional**</u>

Team Teaching

The Five C's

Name _____

Date _____

Theme of team meeting
3 Teaching Verb Tenses

1. Underline how you will do your work at this meeting.
Work in pairs, work in groups of three or four, work alone

2. List below how you now teach verb tenses.

_____

_____

_____

3. List below your dream list of new ways to teach verb tenses. _____

_____

_____

_____

4. Write your action plan for including your new techniques to teach verb tenses. Write what, when, where, how, and why you plan to do this.

_____

_____

_____

5. Discuss with all members of the team your old and new techniques to teach verb tenses. Say what your action plan is for implementing your new ways to teach verb tenses into your lesson plans. Ask others for positive feedback.
Instructional

Team Teaching ♪

Name _____

Date _____

Theme of team meeting
4 Teaching Grammar Effectively

1. Underline how you will do your work at this meeting.
Work in pairs, work in groups of three or four, work alone

2. List below your present techniques for teaching grammar.

_____

_____

_____

3. List below your dream list of new techniques to effectively teach grammar.

_____

_____

_____

4. Write your action plan for including your new techniques for teaching grammar into your lesson plans. Write what, when, where, how, and why you plan to do this.

_____

_____

_____

_____

5. Discuss with all members of the team your old and new techniques for teaching grammar. Say what your action plan is for implementing the new techniques for teaching grammar effectively into your lesson plans. Ask others for positive feedback.

<u>Instructional</u>

Name _____
Date _____
Theme of team meeting
5 Teaching Vocabulary Effectively

1. Underline how you will do your work at this meeting.
Work in pairs, work in groups of three or four, work alone

2. List below your present techniques for teaching vocabulary.

_____
_____
_____

3. List below your dream list of new techniques to effectively teach vocabulary.

_____
_____
_____
_____

4. Write your action plan for including your new techniques for teaching vocabulary into your lesson plans. Write what, when, where, how, and why you plan to do this.

_____
_____
_____
_____

5. Discuss with all members of the team your old and new techniques for teaching vocabulary. Say what your action plan is for implementing the new techniques for teaching vocabulary effectively into your lesson plans. Ask others for positive feedback.

Instructional

Team Teaching

Name _____

Date _____

Theme of team meeting
6 National Standards, the Five C's

1. Underline how you will do your work at this meeting.
Work in pairs, work in groups of three or four, work alone

2. List below the five C's.

_____

3. List the five C's that you teach in your class. Give examples.

_____
_____
_____
_____

4. List below your dream list of new plans-materials-methods that you plan to use to teach the five C's. Include details.

_____
_____
_____
_____
_____
_____

5. Write your action plan for including an expanded and more detailed teaching of the five C's. Write what, when, where, how, and why you plan to do this.

_____
_____
_____
_____

6. Discuss with all of the team members your new plans to teach the five C's. Say what your action plan is for implementing the standards into your lesson plans. Ask others for positive feedback.

<u>Instructional</u>

Team Teaching

The FIVE C's

©2000, Teacher's Discovery

Name _____

Date _____

Theme of team meeting
<u>7</u> Teaching Culture

1. Underline how you will do your work at this meeting.
Work in pairs, work in groups of three or four, work alone

2. List below your present techniques for teaching culture.
_____
_____
_____

3. List below your dream list of new techniques to effectively teach culture.
_____
_____
_____

4. Write your action plan for including your new techniques for teaching culture into your lesson plans. Write what, when, where, how, and why you plan to do this.
_____
_____
_____
_____

5. Discuss with all members of the team your old and new techniques for teaching culture. Say what your action plan is for implementing the new techniques for teaching culture into your lesson plans. Ask others for positive feedback.
<u>Instructional</u>

Team Teaching

Name _____

Date _____

Theme of team meeting
8 Teaching Communicatively

1. Underline how you will do your work at this meeting.
Work in pairs, work in groups of three or four, work alone

2. List below your present techniques for teaching communicatevly.

_____

_____

_____

3. List below your dream list of new techniques to effectively teach communication.

_____

_____

_____

_____

4. Write your action plan for including your new techniques for teaching communicately into your lesson plans. Write what, when, where, how, and why you plan to do this.

_____

_____

_____

_____

5. Discuss with all members of the team your old and new techniques for teaching communicatively. Say what your action plan is for implementing the new techniques for teaching communicatively into your lesson plans. Ask others for positive feedback.

<u>Instructional</u>

©2000, Teacher's Discovery

Name _____
Date _____
Theme of team meeting
9 Team Teaching

1. Underline how you will do your work at this meeting.
Work in pairs, work in groups of three or four, work alone

2. List below your present techniques for teaching as a team.

_____
_____
_____

3. List below your dream list of new techniques to effectively teach as a team.

_____
_____
_____

4. Write your action plan for including your new techniques for team teaching into your lesson plans. Write what, when, where, how, and why you plan to do this.

_____
_____
_____

5. Discuss with all members of the team your old and new techniques for teaching team teaching. Say what your action plan is for implementing the new techniques for team teaching into your lesson plans. Ask others for positive feedback.

<u>Instructional</u>

Name _____

Date _____

Theme of team meeting
<u>10 Multiple Intelligences</u>

1. Underline how you will do your work at this meeting.
Work in pairs, work in groups of three or four, work alone

2. List below your present techniques for teaching multiple intelligences.

_____

_____

_____

3. List below your dream list of new techniques to teach multiple intelligences.

_____

_____

_____

_____

4. Write your action plan for including your new techniques for teaching multiple intelligences into your lesson plans. Write what, when, where, how, and why you plan to do this.

_____

_____

_____

_____

5. Discuss with all members of the team your old and new techniques for teaching multiple intelligences. Say what your action plan is for implementing the new techniques for teaching multiple intelligences into your lesson plans. Ask others for positive feedback.

<u>Instructional</u>

Team Teaching

©2000, Teacher's Discovery

The FIVE C'S

Name _____

Date _____

Theme of team meeting
<u>11 Learning Centers</u>

1. Underline how you will do your work at this meeting.
Work in pairs, work in groups of three or four, work alone

2. List below when and how you presently use learning centers (stations).

_____
_____
_____

3. List below your dream list of new ways of using learning centers with your students.

_____
_____
_____

4. Write your action plan for including your new uses of learning centers into your lesson plans. Write what, when, where, how, and why you plan to do this.

_____
_____
_____

5. Discuss with all members of the team your old and new techniques for implementing learning centers into your classes. Say what your action plan is for implementing the new techniques for using learning centers in your lesson plans. Ask others for positive feedback.

<u>Instructional</u>

Team Teaching

Name _____

Date _____

Theme of team meeting
<u>12 Teaching Songs</u>

1. Underline how you will do your work at this meeting.
Work in pairs, work in groups of three or four, work alone

2. List below your present techniques for teaching songs.

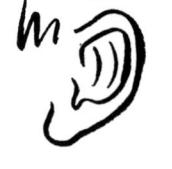

_____

_____

_____

3. List below your dream list of new techniques to effectively teach songs.

_____

_____

_____

4. Write your action plan for including your new techniques for teaching songs into your lesson plans. Write what, when, where, how, and why you plan to do this.

_____

_____

_____

_____

5. Discuss with all members of the team your old and new techniques for teaching songs. Say what your action plan is for implementing the new techniques for teaching songs into your lesson plans. Ask others for positive feedback.
<u>Instructional</u>

Name _____

Date _____

Theme of team meeting
13 Cooperative Learning

1. Underline how you will do your work at this meeting.
Work in pairs, work in groups of three or four, work alone

2. List below your present use of cooperative learning.

_____

_____

_____

3. List below your dream list of new techniques to include cooperative learning.

_____

_____

_____

4. Write your action plan for including your new techniques for using cooperative learning into your lesson plans. Write what, when, where, how, and why you plan to do this.

_____

_____

_____

5. Discuss with all members of the team your old and new techniques for using cooperative learning. Say what your action plan is for implementing the new techniques for cooperative learning into your lesson plans. Ask others for positive feedback.

<u>Instructional</u>

Team Teaching

©2000, Teacher's Discovery

Name _____

Date _____

Theme of team meeting
<u>14 Games</u>

1. Underline how you will do your work at this meeting.
Work in pairs, work in groups of three or four, work alone

2. List below the games you use in your classroom.

_____

_____

_____

3. List below your dream list of new games to use with your classes.

_____

_____

_____

_____

4. Write your action plan for including your new games into your lesson plans. Write what, when, where, how, and why you plan to do this.

_____

_____

_____

_____

5. Discuss with all members of the team your old and new games. Say what your action plan is for implementing the new games into your lesson plans. Ask others for positive feedback.

<u>Instructional</u>

Team Teaching

The Five C's

Name _____

Date _____

Theme of team meeting
<u>15 Supplemental Materials</u>

1. Underline how you will do your work at this meeting.
Work in pairs, work in groups of three or four, work alone

2. List below the supplemental materials you presently use.

_____

_____

_____

3. List below your dream list of new supplemental materials.

_____

_____

_____

_____

4. Write your action plan for including new supplemental materials into your lesson plans. Write what, when, where, how, and why you plan to do this.

_____

_____

_____

_____

5. Discuss with all members of the team your old and new techniques for using supplemental materials. Say what your action plan is for implementing the new supplemental materials into your lesson plans. Ask others for positive feedback.

<u>Instructional</u>

Team Teaching

Name _____

Date _____

Theme of team meeting
<u>16 Listening Activities</u>

1. Underline how you will do your work at this meeting.
Work in pairs, work in groups of three or four, work alone

2. List below the listening activities you presently use.

_____
_____
_____

3. List below your dream list of new listening activities.

_____
_____

_____
_____

4. Write your action plan for including new listening activities into your lesson plans. Write what, when, where, how, and why you plan to do this.

_____
_____

_____
_____
_____

5. Discuss with all members of the team your old and new listening activities. Say what your action plan is for implementing the new listening activities into your lesson plans. Ask others for positive feedback.
<u>Instructional</u>

Team Teaching

Name _____

Date _____

Theme of team meeting
17 Speaking Activities

1. Underline how you will do your work at this meeting.
Work in pairs, work in groups of three or four, work alone

2. List below the speaking activities you presently use.
_____
_____
_____

3. List below your dream list of new speaking activities.
_____
_____
_____

4. Write your action plan for including new speaking activities into your lesson plans. Write what, when, where, how, and why you plan to do this.
_____
_____
_____
_____

5. Discuss with all members of the team your old and new speaking activities. Say what your action plan is for implementing the new speaking activities into your lesson plans. Ask others for positive feedback.

<u>Instructional</u>

Team Teaching

Name _____

Date _____

Theme of team meeting
18 Reading Activities

1. Underline how you will do your work at this meeting.
Work in pairs, work in groups of three or four, work alone

2. List below the reading activities you presently use.
_____
_____
_____

3. List below your dream list of new reading activities.
_____
_____
_____
_____

4. Write your action plan for including new reading activities into your lesson plans. Write what, when, where, how, and why you plan to do this.
_____
_____
_____

5. Discuss with all members of the team your old and new reading activities. Say what your action plan is for implementing the new reading activities into your lesson plans. Ask others for positive feedback.

<u>Instructional</u>

Name _____
Date _____

Theme of team meeting
<u>19 Writing Activities</u>

1. Underline how you will do your work at this meeting.
Work in pairs, work in groups of three or four, work alone

2. List below the writing activities you presently use.

_____

_____

_____

3. List below your dream list of new writing activities.

_____

_____

_____

4. Write your action plan for including new writing activities into your lesson plans. Write what, when, where, how, and why you plan to do this.

_____

_____

_____

_____

5. Discuss with all members of the team your old and new writing activities. Say what your action plan is for implementing the new writing activities into your lesson plans. Ask others for positive feedback.
<u>Instructional</u>

Team Teaching

Name _____

Date _____

Theme of team meeting
20 Technology in the FL Classroom

1. Underline how you will do your work at this meeting.
Work in pairs, work in groups of three or four, work alone

2. List below how and where you are currently using technology in your teaching.

_____
_____
_____

3. List below your dream list of new ways to use technology in your teaching. Include details.

_____
_____
_____
_____
_____

5. Write your action plan for implementing technology into your teaching. Write what, when, where, how, and why you plan to do this.

_____
_____
_____
_____
_____
_____
_____

6. Discuss with all the department members your new plans to use technology in your teaching. Say what your action plan is for implementing technology into your lesson plans. Ask others for positive feedback.

Instructional

Team Teaching

The Five C's

Name _____
Date _____
Theme of team meeting
21 Internet and Culture

1. Underline how you will do your work at this meeting.
Work in pairs, work in groups of three or four, work alone

2. List below how and where you are currently using the Internet to teach culture.

_____
_____

_____

3. List below your dream list of new ways to teach culture on the Internet. Include details.

_____
_____
_____
_____
_____

5. Write your action plan for using the Internet to teach culture. Write what, when, where, how, and why you plan to do this.

_____
_____
_____
_____
_____
_____
_____

6. Discuss with all the department members your new plans to use the Internet to teach culture. Say what your action plan is for including the Internet into your lesson plans. Ask others for positive feedback.
<u>Instructional</u>

Team Teaching

©2000, Teacher's Discovery

Name _____

Date _____

Theme of team meeting
<u>22 TPR</u>

1. Underline how you will do your work at this meeting.
Work in pairs, work in groups of three or four, work alone

2. List below how and where you are currently using TPR in your teaching.

_____
_____
_____

3. List below your dream list of new ways to use TPR in your teaching. Include details.

_____
_____
_____
_____
_____

5. Write your action plan for implementing TPR into your teaching. Write what, when, where, how, and why you plan to do this.

_____
_____
_____
_____
_____
_____
_____

6. Discuss with all the department members your new plans to use TPR in your teaching. Say what your action plan is for implementing TPR into your lesson plans. Ask others for positive feedback.

<u>Instructional</u>

Name _____

Date _____

Theme of team meeting
<u>23</u> Creative Lesson Planning

1. Underline how you will do your work at this meeting.
Work in pairs, work in groups of three or four, work alone

2. List below how and where you are currently using creative lesson planning.

_____

_____

3. List below your dream list of new ways to do creative lesson planning. Include details.

_____

_____

_____

_____

5. Write your action plan for implementing creative lesson planning. Write what, when, where, how, and why you plan to do this.

_____

_____

_____

_____

_____

_____

6. Discuss with all the department members your new plans for using creative lesson planning. Say what your action plan is for implementing creative lesson planning. Ask others for positive feedback.
<u>Instructional</u>

Team Teaching

Name _____

Date _____

Theme of team meeting

<u>24</u> National FL Exam-Practice

1. Underline how you will do your work at this meeting.
Work in pairs, work in groups of three or four, work alone

2. List below how and where you are practicing with your students for the National FL Exams.

_____

_____

_____

3. List below your dream list of new ways to practice creatively for the National FL Exam. Include details.

_____

_____

_____

_____

_____

5. Write your action plan for implementing creative ways to practice for the National FL Exam. Write what, when, where, how, and why you plan to do this.

_____

_____

_____

_____

_____

_____

6. Discuss with all the department members your new plans for creatively practicing for the National FL Exam. Say what your action plan is for implementing the creative practice. Ask others for positive feedback.

<u>Instructional</u>

Team Teaching

Name _____

Date _____

Theme of team meeting

25 AP Practice

1. Underline how you will do your work at this meeting.
Work in pairs, work in groups of three or four, work alone

2. List below how and where you are currently practicing for the AP test in your FL.

_____
_____

3. List below your dream list of new ways to do creative practice for the AP. Include details.

_____
_____
_____
_____

5. Write your action plan for implementing creative practice for the AP. Write what, when, where, how, and why you plan to do this.

_____
_____
_____
_____
_____

6. Discuss with all the department members your new plans for using creative AP practice. Say what your action plan is for implementing your creative plan. Ask others for positive feedback.

Instructional

Team Teaching

Name _____

Date _____

Theme of team meeting
<u>26 FL Testing</u>

1. Underline how you will do your work at this meeting.
Work in pairs, work in groups of three or four, work alone

2. List below how and where you currently test in your classes.

_____
_____
_____

3. List below your dream list of new ways to do creative testing. Include details.

_____
_____
_____
_____
_____

5. Write your action plan for implementing creative testing. Write what, when, where, how, and why you plan to do this.

_____
_____
_____
_____
_____
_____
_____

6. Discuss with all the department members your new plans for using creative testing. Say what your action plan is for implementing your creative testing. Ask others for positive feedback.

<u>Instructional</u>

Team Teaching

The Five C's

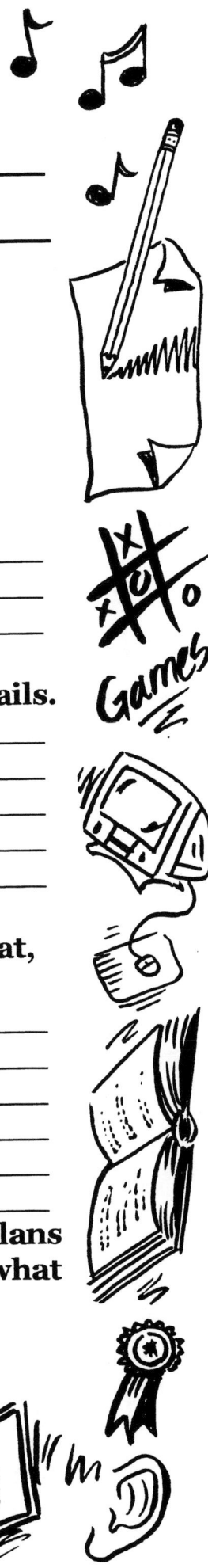

Name _____

Date _____

Theme of team meeting
27 Interdisciplinary Activities

1. Underline how you will do your work at this meeting.
Work in pairs, work in groups of three or four, work alone

2. List below how and where you are currently using interdisciplinary activities in your teaching.

_____

_____

_____

3. List below your dream list of new ways to use interdisciplinary activities in your teaching. Include details.

_____

_____

_____

_____

_____

5. Write your action plan for implementing interdisciplinary activities into your teaching. Write what, when, where, how, and why you plan to do this.

_____

_____

_____

_____

_____

6. Discuss with all the department members your new plans to use interdisciplinary activities in your teaching. Say what your action plan is for implementing interdisciplinary activities into your lesson plans. Ask others for positive feedback.

<u>**Instructional**</u>

Name _____
Date _____
Theme of team meeting
<u>28 Paired Activities</u>

1. Underline how you will do your work at this meeting.
Work in pairs, work in groups of three or four, work alone

2. List below how and where you are currently using paired activities in your teaching.

_____
_____
_____

3. List below your dream list of new ways to use paired activities in your teaching. Include details.

_____
_____
_____
_____

5. Write your action plan for implementing paired activities into your teaching. Write what, when, where, how, and why you plan to do this.

_____
_____
_____
_____
_____

6. Discuss with all the department members your new plans to use paired activities in your teaching. Say what your action plan is for implementing paired activities into your lesson plans. Ask others for positive feedback.
<u>Instructional</u>

Name _____

Date _____

Theme of team meeting
<u>29 Groups of Three or Four</u>

1. Underline how you will do your work at this meeting.
Work in pairs, work in groups of three or four, work alone

2. List below how and where you are currently using groups of three of four in your teaching.

_____

_____

_____

3. List below your dream list of new ways to use groups of three or four in your teaching. Include details.

_____

_____

_____

_____

5. Write your action plan for implementing groups of three or four into your teaching. Write what, when, where, how, and why you plan to do this.

_____

_____

_____

_____

_____

_____

6. Discuss with all the department members your new plans to use groups of three or four in your teaching. Say what your action plan is for implementing small groups into your lesson plans. Ask others for positive feedback.
<u>Instructional</u>

Team Teaching

Name _____

Date _____

Theme of team meeting
30 Videotape Viewing Activities

1. Underline how you will do your work at this meeting.
Work in pairs, work in groups of three or four, work alone

2. List below how and where you use videotape viewing activities in your teaching.

_____
_____
_____

3. List below your dream list of new ways to include videotape viewing activities in your teaching. Include details.

_____
_____
_____
_____

5. Write your action plan for implementing videotape viewing activities into your teaching. Write what, when, where, how, and why you plan to do this.

_____
_____
_____
_____
_____
_____

6. Discuss with all the department members your new plans to use videotape viewing activities in your teaching. Say what your action plan is for implementing videotape viewing activities into your lesson plans. Ask others for positive feedback.

__Instructional__

Name _____

Date _____

Theme of team meeting
<u>31 FL Lab Activities</u>

1. Underline how you will do your work at this meeting.
Work in pairs, work in groups of three or four, work alone

2. List below how and where you are currently using FL lab activities in your teaching.

_____

_____

_____

_____

3. List below your dream list of new ways to use FL lab activities in your teaching. Include details.

_____

_____

_____

_____

5. Write your action plan for implementing FL lab activities into your teaching. Write what, when, where, how, and why you plan to do this.

_____

_____

_____

_____

_____

_____

6. Discuss with all the department members your new plans to use FL lab activities in your teaching. Say what your action plan is for implementing FL lab activities into your lesson plans. Ask others for positive feedback.
<u>Instructional</u>

Team Teaching

Name _____
Date _____
Theme of team meeting
32 Preparing the Student Teacher

1. Underline how you will do your work at this meeting.
Work in pairs, work in groups of three or four, work alone

2. List below how you presently prepare your student teacher.

_____
_____
_____
_____

3. List below your dream list of new ways to creatively prepare your student teacher. Include details.

_____
_____
_____
_____
_____

5. Write your action plan for implementing creative preparation of your student teacher. Write what, when, where, how, and why you plan to do this.

_____
_____
_____
_____

6. Discuss with all the department members your new plans to creatively prepare your student teacher. Say what your action plan is for a creative preparation of your student teacher. Ask others for positive feedback.
__Instructional__

Team Teaching

The FIVE C's

Name _____

Date _____

Theme of team meeting
33 Creative Seating Arrangements

1. Underline how you will do your work at this meeting.
Work in pairs, work in groups of three or four, work alone

2. List below how and where you are currently using creative seating arrangements.

_____
_____
_____
_____

3. List below your dream list of new ways to include creative seating arrangements. Include details.

_____
_____
_____
_____

5. Write your action plan for implementing creative seating arrangements. Write what, when, where, how, and why you plan to do this.

_____
_____
_____
_____
_____
_____

6. Discuss with all the department members your new plans for using creative seating arrangements. Say what your action plan is for implementing creative seating arrangements. Ask others for positive feedback.
Instructional

Team Teaching

Name _____

Date _____

Theme of team meeting
<u>34</u> Effective Discipline

1. Underline how you will do your work at this meeting.
Work in pairs, work in groups of three or four, work alone

2. List below how and where you are currently using effective discipline in your teaching.

_____
_____
_____
_____

3. List below your dream list of new ways to use effective discipline in your teaching. Include details.

_____
_____
_____
_____

5. Write your action plan for implementing effective discipline into your teaching. Write what, when, where, how, and why you plan to do this.

_____
_____
_____
_____

6. Discuss with all the department members your new plans to use effective discipline in your teaching. Say what your action plan is for implementing effective discipline into your lesson plans. Ask others for positive feedback.
<u>Instructional</u>

Name _____

Date _____

Theme of team meeting
35 Teacher-Student Rapport

1. Underline how you will do your work at this meeting.
Work in pairs, work in groups of three or four, work alone

2. List below how your rapport is with your students.

_____
_____
_____
_____

3. List below your dream list of new ways to improve rapport with your students. Include details.

_____
_____
_____
_____

5. Write your action plan for improving your rapport with the students. Write what, when, where, how, and why you plan to do this.

_____
_____
_____
_____
_____

6. Discuss with all the department members your new plans for improving rapport with your students. Say what your action plan is for improving rapport. Ask others for positive feedback.

<u>Instructional</u>

Team Teaching

2000, Teacher's Discovery

Name _____

Date _____

Theme of team meeting
36 Keeping a Positive Attitude

1. Underline how you will do your work at this meeting.
Work in pairs, work in groups of three or four, work alone

2. List below how you now maintain a positive attitude.

_____

_____

3. List below your dream list of new ways to have a positive attitude.

_____

_____

_____

_____

_____

4. Write your action plan for including your new techniques to have a positive attitude. Write what, when, where, how, and why you plan to do this.

_____

_____

_____

5. Discuss with all members of the team your old and new techniques to keep a positive attitude. Say what your action plan is for implementing your new positive attitude. Ask others for positive feedback.

Instructional

Team Teaching

The Five C's

Name _____

Date _____

Theme of team meeting
37 FL in Elementary Schools

1. Underline how you will do your work at this meeting.
Work in pairs, work in groups of three or four, work alone

2. List below how you promote FL in elementary schools.
_____
_____
_____

3. List below your dream list of new ways to promote FL in elementary schools.
_____
_____
_____
_____

4. Write your action plan for including your new techniques to promote FL in elementary schools. Write what, when, where, how, and why you plan to do this.
_____
_____
_____

5. Discuss with all members of the team your old and new techniques to promote FL in elementary schools. Say what your action plan is for implementing your new ways to promote FL in elementary schools. Ask others for positive feedback.

<u>**Promotional**</u>

©2000, Teacher's Discovery

Name _____

Date _____

Theme of team meeting
<u>38</u> FL in Middle Schools

1. Underline how you will do your work at this meeting.
Work in pairs, work in groups of three or four, work alone

2. List below how you now promote FL in middle schools.
_____
_____
_____

3. List below your dream list of new ways to promote FL in middle schools.
_____
_____
_____
_____
_____

4. Write your action plan for including your new techniques to promote FL in middle schools. Write what, when, where, how, and why you plan to do this.
_____
_____
_____
_____

5. Discuss with all members of the team your old and new techniques to promote FL in middle schools. Say what your action plan is for implementing your new ways to promote FL in middle schools. Ask others for positive feedback.
<u>Promotional</u>

Team Teaching

The FIVE C's

Name _____

Date _____

Theme of team meeting
<u>39 FL Newspaper</u>

1. Underline how you will do your work at this meeting.
Work in pairs, work in groups of three or four, work alone

2. List below the format of any FL newspapers your students have done.

_____

_____

3. List below your dream list of new ways to create a FL newspaper.

_____

_____

_____

_____

_____

4. Write your action plan for including your new techniques to create a FL newspaper. Write what, when, where, how, and why you plan to do this.

_____

_____

_____

5. Discuss with all members of the team your old and new techniques to create a FL newspaper. Say what your action plan is for implementing your new ideas for creating a FL newspaper. Ask others for positive feedback.
<u>Promotional</u>

Name _____

Date _____

Theme of team meeting
40 FL Promotional Brochure

1. Underline how you will do your work at this meeting.
Work in pairs, work in groups of three or four, work alone

2. List below how you create any FL promotional brochure.
_____
_____
_____

3. List below your dream list of new ways to create a FL brochure.
_____
_____
_____
_____
_____

4. Write your action plan for including your new techniques for creating a FL brochure. Write what, when, where, how, and why you plan to do this.
_____
_____
_____
_____

5. Discuss with all members of the team your old and new techniques for creating a FL brochure. Say what your action plan is for implementing your new ways for creating a FL brochure. Ask others for positive feedback.

Promotional

Team Teaching

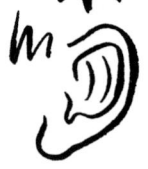

The Five C's

Name _____

Date _____

Theme of team meeting
<u>41</u> FL Week

1. Underline how you will do your work at this meeting.
Work in pairs, work in groups of three or four, work alone

2. List below how you prepare for FL week.

_____

_____

_____

3. List below your dream list of new ways to promote FL week.

_____

_____

_____

_____

_____

4. Write your action plan for including your new techniques for planning FL week. Write what, when, where, how, and why you plan to do this.

_____

_____

_____

_____

5. Discuss with all members of the team your old and new techniques for planning FL week. Say what your action plan is for implementing your new ideas for FL week. Ask others for positive feedback.

<u>**Promotional**</u>

Name _____

Date _____

Theme of team meeting
42 FL Club

1. Underline how you will do your work at this meeting.
Work in pairs, work in groups of three or four, work alone

2. List below how you now plan for FL club.

_____
_____
_____

3. List below your dream list of new ways to plan for FL club._____

_____
_____
_____

4. Write your action plan for including your new techniques for planning FL club. Write what, when, where, how, and why you plan to do this.

_____
_____
_____
_____

5. Discuss with all members of the team your old and new techniques for planning FL club. Say what your action plan is for implementing your new ways for planning FL club. Ask others for positive feedback.
Promotional

Team Teaching

The FIVE C'S

Name _____

Date _____

Theme of team meeting
<u>43</u> <u>Fund Raisers</u>

1. Underline how you will do your work at this meeting.
Work in pairs, work in groups of three or four, work alone

2. List below what you now do for a fund raiser.

_____

_____

_____

3. List below your dream list of new possibilities for fund raisers.

_____

_____

_____

_____

_____

4. Write your action plan for having a new and different fund raiser. Write what, when, where, how, and why you plan to do this.

_____

_____

_____

_____

5. Discuss with all members of the team your old and new techniques for having fund raisers. Say what your action plan is for implementing your new fund raiser. Ask others for positive feedback.

<u>Promotional</u>

Name _____

Date _____

Theme of team meeting
44 Bulletin Boards

1. Underline how you will do your work at this meeting.
Work in pairs, work in groups of three or four, work alone

2. List below how you now create promotional bulletin boards for FL.

_____
_____
_____

3. List below your dream list of new ways to do your bulletin boards to promote FL.

_____
_____
_____
_____
_____

4. Write your action plan for including your new techniques to create promotional bulletin boards for FL. Write what, when, where, how, and why you plan to do this.

_____
_____
_____

5. Discuss with all members of the team your old and new techniques for creating promotional bulletin boards. Say what your action plan is for implementing your new bulletin board ideas. Ask others for positive feedback.

Promotional

Team Teaching

The FIVE C's

Name _____

Date _____

Theme of team meeting
<u>45</u> <u>Student Travel</u>

1. Underline how you will do your work at this meeting.
Work in pairs, work in groups of three or four, work alone

2. List below how you plan student trips and where you go.

_____

_____

_____

3. List below your dream list of new ways to plan student trips.

_____

_____

_____

_____

4. Write your action plan for including your new techniques for planning student trips. Write what, when, where, how, and why you plan to do this.

_____

_____

_____

5. Discuss with all members of the team your old and new techniques for planning student trips. Say what your action plan is for implementing your new ideas. Ask others for positive feedback.

<u>Promotional</u>

©2000, Teacher's Discovery

Name _____

Date _____

Theme of team meeting
<u>46 FL Video Promotion</u>

1. Underline how you will do your work at this meeting.
Work in pairs, work in groups of three or four, work alone

2. List below what videos you use to promote the study of FL.

_____
_____
_____

3. List below your dream list of new videos to promote FL study.

_____
_____
_____
_____
_____

4. Write your action plan for including your new ideas for videos (student made or others) to promote FL study. Write what, when, where, how, and why you plan to do this.

_____
_____
_____
_____

5. Discuss with all members of the team your old and new videos for promoting FL study. Say what your action plan is for implementing your new ideas-videos. Ask others for positive feedback.

<u>**Promotional**</u>

Name _____

Date _____

Theme of team meeting
<u>47</u> FL Honor Society

1. Underline how you will do your work at this meeting.
Work in pairs, work in groups of three or four, work alone

2. List below how you now use your FL honor society to promote FL study.

_____

_____

3. List below your dream list of new ways to use your FL honor society to promote FL study.

_____

_____

_____

_____

4. Write your action plan for including your new ideas for promoting FL through the FL honor society. Write what, when, where, how, and why you plan to do this.

_____

_____

_____

5. Discuss with all members of the team your old and new techniques for promoting FL study using your FL honor society. Say what your action plan is for implementing your new ideas. Ask others for positive feedback.

<u>Promotional</u>

Name _____

Date _____

Theme of team meeting
<u>48</u> Guest Speakers

1. Underline how you will do your work at this meeting.
Work in pairs, work in groups of three or four, work alone

2. List below how you now use guest speakers to promote FL study.

_____

_____

_____

3. List below your dream list of new ways to use guest speakers to promote FL study.

_____

_____

_____

_____

4. Write your action plan for including your new ideas to use guest speakers to promote FL study. Write what, when, where, how, and why you plan to do this.

_____

_____

_____

_____

5. Discuss with all members of the team your old and new ideas for using guest speakers to promote FL study. Say what your action plan is for implementing your new ideas. Ask others for positive feedback.

<u>**Promotional**</u>

©2000, Teacher's Discovery

Name _____

Date _____

Theme of team meeting
<u>49</u> Teacher Observations-Evaluations

1. Underline how you will do your work at this meeting.
Work in pairs, work in groups of three or four, work alone

2. List below how you use the classroom observations-evaluations of the department chairperson to help you.

_____

_____

_____

3. List below your dream list of new ways to use your observations-evaluations to help you improve.

_____

_____

_____

_____

4. Write your action plan for including your new ideas on how to use your observations-evaluations to improve instruction. Write what, when, where, how, and why you plan to do this.

_____

_____

_____

5. Discuss with all members of the team your old and new ideas on using observations-evaluations to improve instruction. Say what your action plan is for implementing your new ideas. Ask others for positive feedback.
<u>**Administration-Faculty-Parents**</u>

Team Teaching

Name _____

Date _____

Theme of team meeting
<u>50</u> Rapport with other Departments

1. Underline how you will do your work at this meeting.
Work in pairs, work in groups of three or four, work alone

2. Describe below the rapport you have with other departments.

_____
_____
_____

3. List below your dream list of new ways improve your rapport with other departments.

_____
_____
_____
_____
_____

4. Write your action plan for including your new techniques for improving your rapport with other departments. Write what, when, where, how, and why you plan to do this.

_____
_____
_____

5. Discuss with all members of the team your old and new techniques for maintaining rapport with other departments. Say what your action plan is for implementing your new ideas. Ask others for positive feedback.
<u>**Administration-Faculty-Parents**</u>

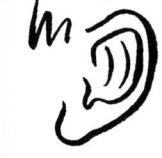

©2000, Teacher's Discovery

Name _____

Date _____

Theme of team meeting
51 Rapport with the Administration

1. Underline how you will do your work at this meeting.
Work in pairs, work in groups of three or four, work alone

2. List below how you are practicing good rapport with the administration.

_____
_____
_____

3. List below your dream list of new ways to help improve rapport with the administration. Include details.

_____
_____
_____
_____

5. Write your action plan for improving and practicing good rapport with your administration. Write what, when, where, how, and why you plan to do this.

_____
_____
_____
_____
_____
_____

6. Discuss with all the department members your new plans to improve rapport with the administration. Say what your action plan is for doing this. Ask others for positive feedback.

Administration-Faculty-Parents

Team Teaching

Name _____

Date _____

Theme of team meeting
52 Rapport with the Parents

1. Underline how you will do your work at this meeting.
Work in pairs, work in groups of three or four, work alone

2. List below how you are practicing good rapport with the parents.

_____

_____

3. List below your dream list of new ways to help improve rapport with the parents. Include details.

_____

_____

_____

_____

5. Write your action plan for improving and practicing good rapport with the parents. Write what, when, where, how, and why you plan to do this.

_____

_____

_____

_____

_____

_____

6. Discuss with all the department members your new plans to improve rapport with the parents. Say what your action plan is for doing this. Ask others for positive feedback.
Administration-Faculty-Parents

Team Teaching

Name _____

Date _____

Theme of team meeting
53 Rapport with the Community

1. Underline how you will do your work at this meeting.
Work in pairs, work in groups of three or four, work alone

2. List below how you are practicing good rapport with the community.

_____
_____
_____

3. List below your dream list of new ways to help improve rapport with the community. Include details.

_____
_____
_____
_____
_____

5. Write your action plan for improving and practicing good rapport with the community. Write what, when, where, how, and why you plan to do this.

_____
_____
_____
_____
_____
_____
_____
_____

6. Discuss with all the department members your new plans to improve rapport with the community. Say what your action plan is for doing this. Ask others for positive feedback.

Administration-Faculty-Parents

Team Teaching

Name _____

Date _____

Theme of team meeting
<u>54 Attendance at FL Conferences</u>

1. Underline how you will do your work at this meeting.
Work in pairs, work in groups of three or four, work alone

2. List below the FL conferences you attended the past year.

_____

_____

3. List below your dream list of FL conferences you want to attend next year. Include details.

_____

_____

_____

_____

5. Write your action plan to attend more FL conferences next year. Write what, when, where, how, and why you plan to do this.

_____

_____

_____

_____

_____

_____

6. Discuss with all the department members your new plans to attend more FL conferences next year. Say what your action plan is for doing this. Ask others for positive feedback.

<u>Professional Development</u>

Team Teaching

The Five C's

Name _____

Date _____

Theme of team meeting

55 Presenting Sessions at FL Conferences

1. Underline how you will do your work at this meeting.
Work in pairs, work in groups of three or four, work alone

2. List below any sessions that you presented this past year at FL conferences.

_____

_____

_____

3. List below your dream list of new sessions to present at FL conferences next year. Include details.

_____

_____

_____

_____

5. Write your action plan for presenting sessions at FL conferences next year. Write what, when, where, how, and why you plan to do this.

_____

_____

_____

_____

_____

_____

_____

_____

6. Discuss with all the department members your new plans for presenting sessions at conferences next year. Say what your action plan is for doing this. Ask others for positive feedback.

Professional Development

Team Teaching

Name _____

Date _____

Theme of team meeting
56 Teacher Travel/Study Abroad

1. Underline how you will do your work at this meeting.
Work in pairs, work in groups of three or four, work alone

2. List below any travel/study programs that you participated in last year.

_____

_____

_____

3. List below your dream list of new travel/study programs in which you plan to participate. Include details.

_____

_____

_____

_____

5. Write your action plan for doing more travel/study programs in the near future. Write what, when, where, how, and why you plan to do this.

_____

_____

_____

_____

_____

_____

_____

6. Discuss with all the department members your new plans for increasing your travel/study abroad. Say what your action plan is for doing this. Ask others for positive feedback.

Professional Development

Team Teaching

The FIVE C's

Name _____
Date _____
Theme of team meeting
<u>57</u> Leadership/Committee Work

1. Underline how you will do your work at this meeting.
Work in pairs, work in groups of three or four, work alone

2. List below any leadership or committee work that you did last year.

_____
_____
_____

3. List below your dream list of new leadership/committees in which you plan to participate. Include details.

_____
_____
_____
_____
_____

5. Write your action plan for increased leadership or committee work. Write what, when, where, how, and why you plan to do this.

_____
_____
_____
_____
_____
_____
_____

6. Discuss with all the department members your new plans for increasing your leadership or committee involvement. Say what your action plan is for doing this. Ask others for positive feedback.
<u>Professional Development</u>

Team Teaching

Name _____

Date _____

Theme of team meeting
<u>58 In-Service Presentations</u>

1. Underline how you will do your work at this meeting.
Work in pairs, work in groups of three or four, work alone

2. List below any in-service presentations you made last year in your school.

_____
_____
_____

3. List below your dream list of new in-service opportunities. Include details.

_____
_____
_____
_____

5. Write your action plan for giving more in-service presentations. Write what, when, where, how, and why you plan to do this.

_____
_____
_____
_____
_____
_____
_____

6. Discuss with all the department members your new plans for more in-service presentations. Say what your action plan is for doing this. Ask others for positive feedback.
<u>Professional Development</u>

Name _____

Date _____

Theme of team meeting
<u>59 Publishing</u>

1. Underline how you will do your work at this meeting.
Work in pairs, work in groups of three or four, work alone

2. List below any materials that you wrote which were published the past year.

_____

_____

3. List below your dream list of materials that you would like to create for publication. Include details.

_____

_____

_____

_____

5. Write your action plan for creating materials to be published. Write what, when, where, how, and why you plan to do this.

_____

_____

_____

_____

_____

_____

_____

6. Discuss with all the department members your new plans for publishing in the future. Say what your action plan is for doing this. Ask others for positive feedback.
<u>Professional development</u>

Team Teaching